Please Don't Die

The World Needs You
Are you Living to Die or Dying to Live?

By

Shree Dembla

Life Coach, Energy Healer
and Consciousness Facilitator

**Please Don't Die
The World Needs You**

Copyrights@2018, Shree Dembla

All rights reserved. No part of this book may be reproduced in any form without permission in writing from the author. Products trademarks mentioned throughout the book remain property of their respective owners.

Paperback ISBN: 978-93-5300-835-2

Disclaimer

No part of this publication may be reproduced or transmitted in any form or by any means, mechanical or electronic, including photocopying or recording, or by any information storage and retrieval system, or transmitted by email without permission in writing from the author and the publisher. While all attempts have been made to verify the information provided in this publication, neither the author nor the publisher assumes any responsibility for errors, omissions, or contrary interpretations of the subject matter herein. This book is for entertainment purposes only. The views expressed are those of the author alone, and should not be taken as expert instruction or command. The reader is responsible for his or her own actions. Neither the author nor the publisher assume any responsibility or liability whatsoever on the behalf of the purchaser or reader of these materials. Any perceived slight of any individual or organization is purely unintentional.

Dedicated to all the Beings seeking

Freedom

Acknowledgement

I would like to express my gratitude to many people who saw me through this book; to all those who provided support, talked things over, read, wrote, offered comments, allowed me to quote their remarks and assisted in the editing, proofreading and design.

I would like to thank my dear friends, mentors, coaches and so much more Gary Douglas & Dr. Dain Heer for being not just the catalyst in my life but being the lapidarists who artistically performed the cutting, grinding, and polishing of the Diamond called me thus enabling me to live my life to the fullest, unleashing my creativity and being me. I would also like to thank Shannon O' Hara and Simone Milasas for being in the world who they are being and for being the contribution in my life that cannot be expressed in words. I am also in Gratitude to Dr. Anthony Mattis for sharing his life with me and the readers and selflessly contributing to this book.

I would like to thank both my parents, my parents that I chose to take birth through (my biological parents) and my parents I chose to nurture me to live fully (my parents in law), my sisters Shaily and Garima, my brother Devansh, my son (in dog's body) Bruno, my friends and my clients.

Above all I would like to express my immense Gratitude to my spouse, Gaurav Dembla, who supported and encouraged me and stood by me even in those times when I refused to stand for myself. It is because of his trust and conviction in me that I am what I am today.

I would like to thank all those who had ever put me into situations where I thought of quitting as this book would not have been possible without them.

Thanks to myself for being who I am and to the anonymous friend for sharing her life with me and allowing and encouraging me to use it to alter many realities.

Last and not the least: I beg forgiveness of all those who have been with me over the course of the years and whose names I have failed to mention.

Forward

If you are someone who would like to live your life fully and yet you have ever thought of quitting on life or running away from current situations or people but you are still alive then this is the book for you.

This book is not about the practical research on suicide and case studies and why and how about suicide. Frankly, I am surprised that beside the fact that I have been desiring to write a book since years and now when I am really sitting down to write one, first one that is shaping up is about Suicide. Yet, what is right about this that I am not getting currently?

Though, I have always been a positive person, like those AGONY AUNTS type, who are always solving problems and making everyone happy. I didn't even realize that I had a constant struggle going on inside me since ever. I don't even remember since how long I have been having the suicidal thoughts. Now when they are gone, I can distinguish what peace and space is and what noise and thoughts were. Most of the time if not always, I had these constant thoughts or voices in my head telling me that I should run away, I should leave, I should either leave the house, leave my family or leave the world. Mostly, they would start right after I will get up in the morning , would get louder when no one would be around, like when I would be cooking food , driving or be in my cabin all by myself. And as they were almost always there I didn't find any need to talk to someone or take any professional help. Professional help anyways was completely out of question also because it is such a taboo in our society that I didn't want to be labeled as psycho or crazy or paagal. Managing the voices inside seemed easier than answering the weird questions, projections and judgments of people around. Mainly, all the times when I was in situations when people around me would be angry either on me or on each other or fight or shout, it will trigger the suicidal thoughts and I would start thinking that I must go away from here by either running away or by committing suicide. I would spend hours visualizing running away from my house and creating a new reality or ways to commit suicide and wonder who would miss me?

Reading this might come as a shock to people who know me as I have never shared this with anyone as talking about committing suicide is considered weakness and weak is the last thing I would like to be judged as, so I would rather plan and plot it and finally shock the world with the news rather than telling anybody as I had this point of view that no one will understand and they will start lecturing me and giving me gyan instead of care and support and freedom.

By this time, if you are still reading this, you must be wondering that, what happened that made me so vulnerable that I finally ended up writing a book about something that I did not even share with anyone all these years. What happened that made me break all my barriers and shackles and eventually made me choose me and be me (the vulnerable, invincible me) and this book came into existence.

Not for me but for you. Yes, you, the one reading this book. Had it not been for you, I would have not been here on the planet. I chose to stay as I got the awareness that I need to share this message that I am about to share with you. So thank you for being here on the planet. It may not make any logical sense to you right now yet by the time you complete this book, you would know that it is because of you that I am alive and that is the contribution you are to my life, that I had to live for you to read this book.

That day, just like any other day I reached my center to start the Miracles I create daily. She called me up, my client. "I did it, I said it all, I am free now, anything is possible, they cannot suppress me anymore, no one can suppress me now", she said. She was sounding different. There was confidence and enthusiasm in her voice compared to the women she was when she first came to meet me. Fiddling with her duppatta, not looking into my eyes when I was talking to her, fumbling while telling me how wrong she was and how she never does anything right and she wish she can make everyone happy but no matter how hard she tries she ends up doing something that upsets people around her, especially her husband.

Regretting that as much as she is trying to make him happy, he is getting more and more upset with her each day. She busted into tears saying, "I don't deserve to live. I am worthless. I should have died long time back." Our first meeting flashed at the back of my mind.

Wow! You sound different girl. I AM different, she replied (emphasizing on am). I can't thank you enough. I love you and I want to meet you. It wasn't for the first time that I was hearing my client saying this but there was something immensely different about the energy she was in, which made me inquisitive to meet her and I immediately agreed to meet her as I really wanted to know what happened? She came over immediately as she wanted to share something which she thought no one else other than me would listen with "no judgment". Ok, I am all ears, I said. And what she shared with me shook me.

About the Author

With several years of practice, Shree Dembla has worked with an eminent passion for being a catalyst for change for many. She is a Life Coach, Energy Healer, Past Life Regression; Future Progression; Age Regression; Inner Child & Life between Life Therapist, Motivational Speaker, Author and Access Consciousness Facilitator. It is her passion to empower people to free themselves from the shackles of their past and take charge of their present thus, recreating a beautiful future.

She has always been a seeker. At the age of eight, she wrote this poem:

> *"If who I am is what I have and what I have is lost, then who am I?*
>
> *If who I am is people around me and people around me are gone, then who am I?*
>
> **If who I am is the work I do and the work I do is over, then who am I?**
>
> **If who I am is the body I have and the body I have dies, then who am I?"**

Her mother was amazed to see an eight-year-old having questions like these and told her that, the road to self-discovery would not be that easy. She has to do tapasya (hard work) for lifetimes and even then only if she is lucky some Guru (teacher) may bless her by giving her this wisdom. She took her advice (literally) and never stopped looking for answers and thus practiced many modalities seeking who is she? Luckily she found Access Consciousness and got the awareness that if she could write such a poem at eight, she was already there. She always knew that she is an Infinite Being beyond what she has, whom she is with, what she does and even beyond her body. Not just that, she knew the art of being in question.

With Post Graduation in Marketing from U.K she worked with many organizations alongside her studies. She won many accolades on her name like MDRT (Million Dollar Round Table) an Oscar of the insurance industry and C.E.O Council for years. Drifting from such a lucrative career, she chose to follow her inner instinct of training and healing the individuals and organization to realize their true potential and add richness and value to their lives.

In her journey from a financial consultant to a Miracle Worker, she has discovered that she has infinite potencies and natural talent to bring a miraculous shift in people's reality by healing them and empowering them with her magical tools and techniques. Over these years Shree has helped many of her clients to alter their reality beyond their imagination be it healing diseases, getting free from addictions and phobias, coming out of abusive relationships, creating new beautiful relationships, beautifying existing communions, making more money, getting fame and experiencing more ease and joy in life.

Today, Shree is inspiring and motivating thousands of people worldwide to recognize their potential and accomplish a prosperous future.

Contents

Disclaimer...iii

Acknowledgement...v

Forward.. vii

About The Author..xii

Chapter 1...

   That Day When She Would Have Gone....................1

Chapter 2...

   It Was Just The Tip Of The Iceberg.....................24

Chapter 3...

   Unspoken Invisible Causes Of Suicide................. 30

Chapter 4...

   What To Do When You Have Suicidal Thoughts?............. 62

Chapter 5...

   When Someone You Know Has Suicidal Tendency...........70

Chapter 6...

   Coping With Loved One's Demise (Dr. Anthony Mattis) 76

Chapter 7...

   Myths Around Suicide................................... 84

Epilogue...

   Please Don't Die, The World Needs You................92

Chapter 1
That Day When She Would Have Gone....

It was a usual day, the only thing different about that day was that it was her birthday. She slept at 3:00 am in the morning talking to friends and receiving birthday wishes till 1:00 am and then having some conversations with her hubby and then just lying in her bed trying to sleep. She was woken up early morning by the knock on her door by her mother in law, waking them up for the Pooja as they must do the Traditional Pooja before she leave her house for work especially on special occasion like birthday.

Right after the pooja, she paced into the kitchen and started with the action packed routine– cooking breakfast for everyone and serving it; Preparing tiffins and packing them; preparing herself mentally for the meetings in the office while quickly completing her household chores and along with all this she had to take her mother in law for shopping today as there was something that has to be bought today itself and she shouldn't forget to buy dadi's (grandmother in law) list when she takes her mother in law for shopping and while plotting it all into her mind to the perfection and making sure that the food is tasty, on time and served fresh and hot, office is managed and the work assigned to her must be completed on time and everyone's demand is fulfilled. She wondered, what is so happy about this Birthday? Why do people even say Happy Birthday?

By 9:00 am in the morning her brain has already reached the optimum capacity to process any new information, she was already exhausted, mentally as well as physically. Sleep deprivation; bombardment of birthday messages from everywhere; physical activity of cooking, packing, serving food; pressure of work at office and planning a family outing at night with family members was already too much to overwhelm her. And right then her usual tape recorder triggered (note that this will add additional messages to the brain and worsen the mental and emotional state) , the usual voice in her head that tells her how pathetic she is, how her life sucks, no one understands her, everyone is mean and so on.

Once again she was sick, sick of everyone and everything around her. She was tired of  people fighting with each other and her. She was tired of everyone making her wrong. She was tired of everyone judging everyone. She was tired of proving that she is a good person, a good daughter, a good wife, a good daughter in law, a good human being etc. etc. She was done with all the fights in and around her. Enough of dragging it for one more day she thought. Enough of proving to the world that her life rocks while it really doesn't. Her head was bursting with her own thoughts and also vibrations/awareness of thoughts in other people's head. She was sick of the hypocrisy of the world and even herself and then she decided to Quit. She was just not interested in life if this is how it's going to be.

It was her birthday and she didn't live even a moment of it for herself, the way she would like to, no one even asked her how would she like to spend her day. She woke up early for doing family rituals beside the fact that she could not sleep till 3 last night followed by taking her mother in law for shopping (who was busy fighting with her father in laws on phone about the Grand Mother in Law all the while) and then trying to create a family outing (a mission impossible).

Climax - Dadi was bribed with a promise to take her out for a movie to allow the mother in law to go shopping and now being a weekend movie tickets are not available!! Which the other family members were worried will upset Dadi, she spoke with Dadi and set her up with a second promise of taking her to her favourite restaurant and now her father in law doesn't want to go out for Dinner as he is angry and upset with Mother in Law & Grand Mother in Law and her husband is angry at his father for being angry with his mother (i.e. the grand-mother in law). And on top of all this her kids do not want to go to Dadi's favourite restaurant. (Truly what the f*ck??) One can't stand the other. One agrees the other disagrees. She convinces one and now someone else is upset for something else and the heat started building up. Just because she was supposed to be this calm, composed, good listener, wise one, everyone would come to her and complaint about the other and she was aware that all she had to do was - nod her head and say "Yes, you are right, they are like this only" to each one of them but sometimes she would miss, sometimes she would forget the simple process – "Yes, you are right they are like this only." And then guess what? She will become wrong. She would be accused of being biased and not understanding things as they are and she would curse herself for skipping a simple process of nodding her head and saying "yes you are right, they are like this only." And somehow she was tired of this too. She couldn't take it anymore; she was tired of all thoughts in her head, all the replay of conversations she was hearing since morning. She couldn't take it anymore so she opened her husband's cupboard and took out the bottle of whisky. It was just half filled so she gulped it and finished it. Right after that, she just threw herself on my bed and fell asleep. After a while she was woken up by a phone call by someone special, the love of her life- her husband. Someone whom she thought understands her more than she understood herself, (can you sense the amount of projections and expectation she has on this person?) and he tried. He asked her – "why are you sounding so upset?" and she replied, "forget it there is no point telling anything to anyone" and he said, "You can tell me, I will listen" and she said "No, You won't, you will just listen a little and then you will get angry at me". He assured he won't. To which she started telling him the entire thing and he started giving her his points of view and eventually, it didn't seem like going anywhere but to anger, rage, confusion and upset. So she decided to end it all.

Her funda was simple, she was living in this lala land where two people can have different opinions or points of view, yet they can be ok about it. Where people are sensitive towards what the other person can hear and not what they think is right. Where no one is right or wrong but they are just being through different situations, circumstances, energy level and imprints of past which does not define them anyways as they can always choose to change, thus, there is no point judging anyone. BUT she failed. It's a lie. It's a fantasy she was living in and no matter how many efforts she make it's not going to happen, she concluded and if this is the world I am living in (where parents expects their kids to be the puppet in their hands but cannot go out for dinner with their own mother, I am not interested anymore, she told to herself. The more she would show people the possibility of her vision or perhaps of her awareness of what our world can be the more they will prove her wrong and show how bad the world around them is. And she would wonder that - If everyone is judging the world around them as bad then are they not the world around someone else, Who is judging them as bad too and does that not make all of us eventually bad? And what is good or bad anyways, bad in whose parameters, who decided the benchmark for this good or bad?

But we are not suppose to ask questions here we are just supposed to agree and keep repeating as a parrot the "Mool Mantra" to survive- "Yes you are right. They are like this only."

And once again she forgot to say the lifesaving line. But this time she wasn't sorry. She was sick. She was tired and she was willing to die. She picked up her car keys, left the house and drove rashly you know why? Because that one person whom she "expected" would understand her got rather angry at her and didn't respond to her the way she "expected" him to and rather told her that if you want to die please go ahead. "What happened, you didn't go to die?" his words kept hammering her head. So, she took on granting his wish on her Birthday.

And she had all these ideas in her head on how to end her life. She had many ideas by the way because it wasn't her first time. She had been contemplating committing suicide since long. She has googled about it too many times earlier. Funny thing is even those who are thinking to commit suicide Google for easiest way to commit suicide or the fastest way or least painful way. Lolz.

Anyways. So she was out of her house, thus there was no place for hanging herself and she had no access to any effective poison, she didn't want to try those stupid rat or cockroach poisons as one they don't even work on rats and cockroaches so didn't want to waste her precious first attempt and secondly, she had been living a life of useless rat (Just being used for experiments by & for others) and spineless cockroach (not taking a stand for anything), thus she shouldn't die their death at least. At least her death must have some ease, joy and glory (It's a pun there is no ease, joy and glory in quitting). Anyways, so she was thinking of banging her car into a truck or buying a paper cutter from a stationary shop for slitting her wrist. She was continuously driving her car rashly, highway after highway while analyzing and introspecting all this. Suddenly the empty indication of the petrol caught her attention and she parked her car on the side. First she took out all her anger by hitting her hand on the car window and even head for number of times and then she told herself that she is strong enough, not to cry and then she cried & howled for a good while and then she begged the universe to show her another possibility and create a different reality for her.

Her mobile battery was running low and she started receiving calls from home which she had no intention to pick up and then her phone was off. She sat their evaluating her next step, concluding that love is crap, everyone is bothered about their own ego and if this is how her life is, it is just not worth it. She couldn't think of going to some friend or relative as they will try to use the situation to make their own brownie point by counseling her and then sending her home yet proving how good they are and how she should fit into this mad reality. She had nowhere to go and almost no one to call as the one she "expected" the most from has already asked her to go commit suicide. So the situation was simple there was just one way possible and that was the way OUT. But as she was about to restart her car to move towards the stationary shop before the shops close down to buy a paper cutter and then slit her wrist and enjoy her slow death as all her blood slowly comes out of her body.

That time it really looked like a fascinating thought to her.

And right at that time, she almost heard my voice telling her, "Please don't die, the world needs you." (I kept telling her this in her session when she was crying and wanted to die but these aren't my lines. In one of my classes with Dr. Dain Heer, a beautiful person and co-founder of Access Consciousness, I went to him and told him that I would have died if Access would not have come into my life and he reverted, "Aww, please don't die the world needs you." Before that moment I personally never realized that I am so valuable for the planet and I can impact so many beings on the planet. and since then it became my reminder to be a contribution to the world and also my Pet Phrase.

Anyways, (coming back to her now) her eyes were filled with tears but this time; these tears were not of helplessness or hopelessness but of gratitude. She remembered how Dr. Dain Heer also planned to commit suicide and then eventually ended up receiving Access Bars Session and then meeting Gary and his whole life changed and she thought that if he would have not received his bars and not have chosen to stay, so much magic that he has created would not have been created on the planet. She remembered me telling her, how he said that to me in the Energetic Synthesis of Being class (ESB) sometimes back. "Please don't die, the world needs you."

She recalled me telling her, how even I wanted to end my life once but I didn't and I had been so thankful to myself for choosing to live, every time I made someone smile or laugh or wiped their tears or appreciated or complimented them or given a healing hug to anyone or touched anyone to heal their issues or shown them a different possibility or shown them how powerful they are. All this would not have been possible if I would not have chosen to live beside the agony. If I would not have made myself realize that I am greater than any situation. All these people that I have touched over the years are already living the life that I am aware is possible and yet they get sucked by the trauma and drama of life as I do too but just because they have done it once, they have at least once learnt to realize that they are greater than any stupid that didn't value them, they can always recreate it. Many of them are still recreating it for themselves and for others. This brought a smile on her face. It reminded her of the story of the 100th monkey that I once told her.

Some scientists conducted a study of macaque monkeys on the Japanese island of  Koshima in 1952. These scientists observed that some of these monkeys learned to wash sweet potatoes, and gradually this new behavior spread through the younger generation of monkeys—in the usual fashion, through observation and repetition. The researchers observed that once a critical number of monkeys was reached, i.e., the hundredth monkey, this previously learned behavior instantly spread across the water to monkeys on nearby islands and the new generation that came, came with the awareness. I have heard them saying in various modalities that we are working for the 100th monkey. Now, that number might be different for humans. I wonder what that number would be. When we are all operating from no judgment of self and others to a degree that the new ones that come gets the environment conducive for their potencies and truly BE themselves.

She remembered my words and she was relieved; it is happening, the world is changing. People have started touching lives of others. Many People she knows are now doing it, on their own. Very soon our next generation will be unstoppable, trauma-drama free, possibility instilled magical beings who naturally believe in ease, joy and glory instead of trauma, drama and agony until then I am not giving up, she told to herself. I am not giving up for stupid people who do not value me and who are not choosing for themselves. In that moment she made fresh choices. Choice to be authentic to herself no matter what, Choice to be brutally honest to herself, Choice to be vulnerable, Choice of never giving up (As Gary always says, Never give up, Never give in, Never quit).

She began to be aware of what happens when a person commits suicide. It was like watching 3D version of movies like Casper etc. She observed how most of the thoughts she was having of ending up the life were not even hers. She was aware of so many past lives where she had slit her wrist, hanged herself, threw herself in front of the train or in well and how her energy body was still carrying the imprints of them, all which would automatically trigger the suicidal thoughts every time she would experience a situation similar to the one which made her past life personality commit suicide. She was aware of so many entities around her speaking those thoughts in her head and dancing with glory that she is going to join their gang soon. She was aware of millions of people on the planet thinking about quitting on life.

And the moment she got aware of it all, suddenly everything got peaceful. She didn't have to die. It would not even be worth it as choosing that would either make her a part of these stuck entities or make her reincarnate again and again and again, until she gets that she has a choice, she always did. She had a choice to say NO to people when she really wanted to but she didn't. She had a choice to do what her heart desired. She had a choice to leave the energy suckers of her life. She had to choice to speak up every time she suppressed her voice. She had a choice to dance and sing and speak and let her voice be heard even if it would attract judgment of few. She had a choice to be in allowance to their judgment, rather receive it with grace as they were never judging her, they were always judging themselves against her.

"I would rather kill then Die", she said to herself. No, no.. She was not preparing herself to literally kill anyone, everyone she was upset with were the people she loves yet she recalled a fable that I once told her.

Once upon a time a saint met a snake on his way. The saint gave the lesson of non violence to the snake and preached him that killing anyone adds to the karmas so he should never harm or kill anyone in order to be free from the cycle to birth and death. The snake learnt his lesson well and promised the saint that he will never harm or kill anyone. On his way back the saint saw the same snake again, but this time he was brutally beaten up. He was bleeding and bruised and almost lifeless. Saint was shocked. He enquired. What happened? You only asked me to never kill anyone the snake replied and see my condition now. I asked you not to kill, the saint replied, but I never asked you to stop hissing. Truly how many of us have even stopped hissing because someone implanted this into us that we must be nice and good and we confused that with being at the effect of others, becoming a door mat and to be killed (energetically if not physically). You cannot create a new reality with the point of view that it is me against others yet you had been missing one very important link in practicing oneness and that is YOU. You have been excluding yourselves out from your life since almost ever. You have been told that until the other person is not cursing you or beating you, it is not an abuse but if anything is being done to you to stop you from Being you, it's an abuse.

Right then she chose to be herself, to be the killing energy if that is what she needs to be herself. No matter how shocking it gets for others. She started her car and searched for a car charger. Charged her phone and without any hesitation attended the call. He yelled at her (her husband) "come home right now where ever you are" to which she replied, "I will not take this and I refuse to talk if you want to talk like this" and disconnected the phone. They called again and this time they were apologetic (her in laws) and she freely took out all the frustrations of all those years without any filters. She was beyond the right or wrong. She didn't have the fear of being judged anymore. She was just being herself, totally vulnerable. For the first time ever in her life, she experienced freedom.

When she left her place she had apprehensions, "where would I go and what would I do" as all her original documents were at home. Yet as that evening ended, it did not matter, nothing mattered. All that mattered was that she was breathing and her fresh promise to herself that as long as she was breathing she will truly live, she will be herself. She is not going to bend, cut, curb, reduce, shrink or suppress herself for anyone else be it those whom she had expectations from because now, no more expecting from others. She clearly communicated to everyone involved that now no one can control her, neither by anger nor by tears. She too has a voice and she will voice it. She will not suppress her self-expression and take medicines and therapies for thyroid, stress, anxiety and sleeping. Enough of living a pathetic life of being a victim, she is not a victim anymore.

As she reached home and lied down she asked the angels "What's right about all  this?"And she got awareness that Miracles do not always show up the way we expect them to, because of all her healing and the new choices she was making and the kind of life she was asking for, Universe has gifted her a new life on her birthday. She also got this urge to share it with me and I knew that this Miracle can touch many lives. How many people out there make it to live after a strong suicidal attack? How many are aware why are they having such thoughts on a regular basis? How many knows what's beside and beyond suicide? How many have someone like Dr. Dain Heer or me, to say to them "Please don't die, the world needs you."

So if you are thinking of committing suicide or if you have ever thought of quitting on life or if you would do that ever in the future please, please, please remember this. Please don't die, the world needs you.

What if you are an amazing being, just the way you are and just the way you are not? What if your unique talents and abilities are the need of the hour? 

What if the situation that you are concluding is too much to handle is the door to a different possibility? What is possible my friend for the planet if you do not give yourself up for anyone no matter what? What else is possible if you stop focusing on the pile of shit that you have made so significant that you believe that you need to sort this up to live your life? What if, all you need to do is to just recognize that you have wings, flutter your wings and fly over that pile of shit?

What if you are never wrong? What if that what you consider as your wrongness is rather a strongness? What if that for which you had been made wrong all your life, is the gift that you have?

Chapter 2
It Was Just The Tip Of The Iceberg

Suicide or Suicidal thoughts are just the tip of the iceberg. There is a lot underneath it. In the moment of "NIRVANA" which was the pause just  before the moment when she finally chose death, she had no fear of it, she had no inhibition of what will happen to people behind and she was totally choosing for herself, many incidences of her life flashed in front of her. She saw glimpses of her parents fights that use to lead to either one of them attempting to suicide or cursing why they are alive or wanting to go away and as being out of relationship didn't seem like an option to them somehow so it meant going away from the world perhaps and wishing that something happens to them and they go away and then the other person would realize their value.

May be this is how the idea of going away got implanted into her system. She was biomimetically mimicking her parents' reality of life (which was secretly hoping to die ironically).

Then she went to the time when she was so heartbroken that she was actually anticipating suicide and  thinking of committing suicide as there didn't seems to be any other option and right when she was paying very serious thoughts to it she got a news that their neighbor's servant has committed suicide (he had put himself on fire and jumped from the third floor) and the police had come and investigating and there was a suicide note that said that he is sick and tired of this life and he hear voices that tell him that he should end his life.

That time she could not distinguish that these voices in her head or thoughts in her head that's says "you should die", "you cannot live anymore", "this life isn't worth it", "no one understands you here" etc. were not even hers. (Please note that if you hear voices in your head that talks to you in second person, pause and ask who is it? As you don't talk to you and address you as "you", you address yourself as "I", right? Then who is it??) They were so real and yet perhaps the news of his suicide was a message from the Universe to consider what she was not considering that she didn't really wanted at that time. She loved her parents immensely and didn't want them to go through investigation and interrogation of police just because she didn't get a desired result in life. She realized that they will be left behind to answer weird, stupid and cruel questions of people all their life. All the conversations that were happening around her about the servant who committed suicide and the police investigation made her realize that if she would have committed suicide people would not have understood that she was in pain but would have made stories around her being a bad or loose character and poked her parents for the same and she loved her parents enough to not let them go through such humiliation so she gathered herself up and chose to live. (Though all that was still unhealed and was affecting her relationships and her way of being when she came to me as a client at the first time).

She so reminded me of myself, sometime back even I was like this. Have you heard the phrase, my way or the highway? My

high was suicide. Every time something would not show up my way, in my head I would immediately go to either I should run away from here or I should commit suicide. And all of this by the way was only happening in my head (it was a secret that I was living), in this reality I was living a jhakaas life, everyone was happy with me, I was best in all parameters of performance be it academics, profession, relationships or conduct. Yet that perfectionism was killing me inside as I had to maintain that perfect image all the time.

Coming back to her, in that moment of Nirvana she also remembered all her fights with her husband which would easily put her to the thoughts of either running away or committing suicide. She also remember all the other fights which were not with her directly but between people around her in which she had to be personally involved and she would think that – "if this is what life is where everyone is either fighting with you or with each other, then I am not interested". All this was actually flashing at a very fast speed and that's the difference between the thoughts and the awareness.

And all the above was just the tip of the iceberg what was underneath was massive. So what was it?

Chapter 3
Unspoken Invisible Causes Of Suicide

Chapter 3.1
Imprints of all the past lives when one had committed suicide

Yes we have lived before this and we have had many lives and there is almost nothing that we haven't done and nothing we haven't been – the good, the bad, and the ugly. In that moment, she got flashes of lives when she died by hanging herself, slitting her wrist, jumping in front of a moving train, jumping in the well etc.

Which made her wonder that the basic perception of people around suicide is that the souls of the beings who commit suicide, do not go to the light and they keep hanging around, right?

She asked, "I was here in this life about to commit suicide watching my  documentary on how many ways I have committed suicide prior to this life." If I had committed suicide, am I not supposed to be hanging around in some past moment?

This can be explained. A part of you that wanted to die to have a new life fragments and move ahead and a part of you that wanted to see who will suffer by your death or have any attachments what so ever with that life, stays behind. But that part kind of keeps hanging around till this part of you doesn't get the awareness which helps liberate all the other stuck bits. As its only then, you either heal yourself and all fragments or you just give up your immortal soul (I highly recommend attending the Foundation class of Access Consciousness for more clarity on this) and choose to be fully present and just be the infinite being you truly are with no past imprints and thus no impact of any past on the future and thus total choice, which makes all those fragments free.

1. Promises, Vows, Oaths

We have already discussed that we have had many lives before this one and many of us have made promises etc. to many other beings and to our own selves in the lives before and we are bound by those promises. Also, many times we have past vows, oaths etc. around those situations and people that we get stuck with, which eventually make us suicidal. Clearing the promises, vows, oaths and also clearing everywhere we had been causally incarcerated with those, alters everything. (Please refer to page no. 109 for more details on how the clearing statements work.)

So mainly we do not experience the freewill of our choice because of the Oaths, Vows, Promises etc we have made in our past or any curse that we have made bigger than ourselves or all

the other ways we have been stuck or committed to any patterns or persons.

The underline cause of depression leading to suicidal tendency can also be some promises , vows, oaths, commitments made to someone in this life or some other past life which the person feel bounded to and now the circumstances have changed and the desire to fulfill the promise is no more there but the being still feels bound to do certain things or be with someone they do not wish to do or be with anymore and most of the time such people get abused as every time you go against your will or awareness you weaken your own energy or aura and this can be taken advantage of by the other person. This is very common in marriages or lovers who were husbands in previous life but are neither marrying in this life nor leaving but just abusing physically or financially or traumatizing emotionally. Clearing the promises, vows, oaths etc with such person frees the person and you begin to see the possibilities which were not available earlier. If you are or have been in such situation or with such person, I highly recommend doing the below clearing as much as you may require to change the energy. Just keep reciting it and you will begin to see the magic of it. Many of my clients are now living a different reality just by using the tool below. However, do not have an expectation or do not go into thinking what will this do. As you clear the past promises, you will start experiencing freedom in your relationships and your life. You can also do it with your relationship that are working to make them even more beautiful. I do it for my husband everynight before I sleep, this somehow maintains the freshness in my relationship.

How many oaths, vows, fealities, commealties, swearings, commitments, promises and contracts do you have to everything you have oaths, vows fealities, commealties, swearings, commitments, promises and contracts to throughout all times, space, dimensions and realities, and bodies, minds and lifetimes that keeps you from having total choice as your reality? All of those, will you please revoke, recant, rescind, reclaim, renounce, denounce, destroy and uncreate them all?

<u>Right and wrong, good and bad, POD and POC, all 9, shorts, boys and beyonds.</u>

2. Curses

Our words create our world and many times we use them so vaguely without even realizing that we may be bounding the other person and our self by the virtue of our words and we may end up cursing the person or even our self. Curses until healed or until you get the awareness and you choose to free yourself from all past ties and realize that you are an infinite being who can never be bounded, continues lifetime after lifetime. I have had clients who had been going through mysterious physical conditions, emotional traumas, psychological and /or psychiatric treatment since years with no improvement, living a totally different reality just after few sessions of releasing curse. Generally, the curses prevail lifetime after lifetime because of the ignorance of believing oneself as a finite being without power and of one's judgment of oneself as less than the one cursing them thus being at the effect of curser. For years human beings have been trapped in the trauma and drama of the cycle of life and birth and cause and effect reality and incarnating again and again. Is it time to be free from all these?

For years human beings didn't realize that they have the choice to Eliminate and Eradicate the Allergic Solidification of the Responses of Disagreement & Curses and be free. It is really just a choice. So <u>everywhere you had been cursed and everywhere you cursed someone would you please revoke, recant, rescind, reclaim, renounce, denounce, destroy and uncreate it all? (all you need to do is say yes)</u>

<u>Right and Wrong, Good and Bad, POD and POC, All 9, Shorts, Boys and Beyonds.</u>

Chapter No. 3.2
Implants

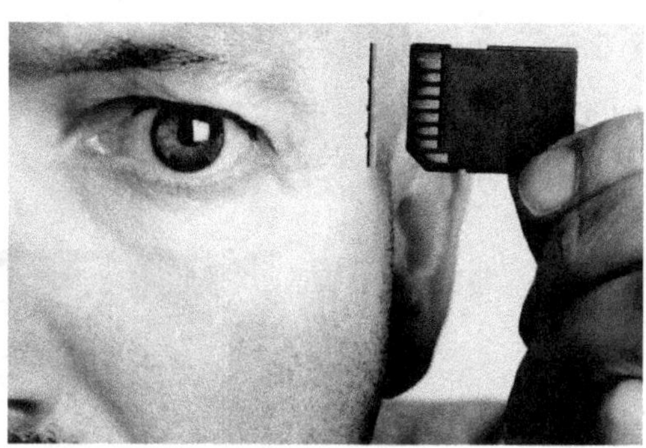

Every time we either aligned or agreed to or resisted or reacted to anyone's points of views it gets implanted to our system like an invisible chip or program that activates only when a similar situation show up. Don't we end up doing the same thing that we disliked or resisted in our parents, when we get to that age or get into a similar situation? It is an implant working not just of this life but many life times. Imagine how many implants are running your life? Are you ever truly you?

There are so many implants that distract us from being totally present and taking a charge of our life. Thus, they may also be termed as Distracter Implants. You can't fix those things because you never created them at the first place, you got implanted. Distracter implants are designed to get you into judgment of you, not into handling what's actually there. You would be surprised to know what are some of these implants, anger, Fear, Blame, Shame, Regret, Guilt, Love, Hate, Sex, Jealousy, Peace, Life, Death, Doubt etc.

That basically sums up almost everything about suicide isn't it? You 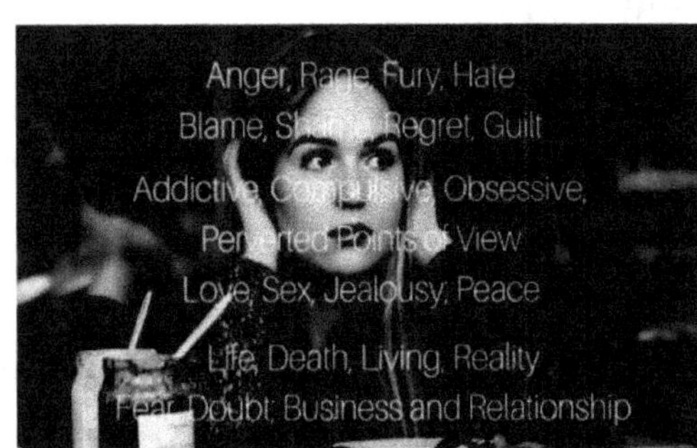

must be wondering that why are we implanted with all these. The answer is simple, to control you. If you are not implanted with something that keeps you distracted from being you, then you will start questioning, you will start creating, you will be the change, you will then be different and if everyone start being different then the status quo will be threatened.

But how does distracter implants lead to suicidal thoughts? They keep you distracted from being you and lead you to resolve something which cannot be resolved at the first place. You had been trying to understand all these and control all these or forcing yourself to be controlled by all these which eventually leads you to constantly judge yourself or others as right or wrong and not be in allowance of yourself or them, just as how you are or they are. And all these lead to so much frustration that you finally decide to give up, give in and quit.

The underneath cause of any suicidal thought is the constant thought pattern of being made wrong by self or others and eventually suicide happens when the person choose to give up on being wronged or when someone is not being themselves since long and the being cannot take it anymore. The important thing to note here is that we are constantly being made wrong on the parameters of these distracter implants.

The awareness of these create the possibility of freedom as you begin to realize that everything you have made significant is not significant, nothing is significant and everything is CHOICE.

Blame, Shame, Fear & Guilt

Sometimes people do not wish to live anymore because they have a secret that they cannot carry anymore. Most of the time, it is something they think they were not supposed to do and they have done it and now they are dreading what will happen if people or someone (they are scared should not get to know about it) will get to know about it. Their mind starts building stories around it, showing them all the worst possible outcomes.

What if guilt, blame, shame, fear etc. are not real? What if they are just implants, implanted into you to control you? What are you not willing to be judged as that if you were willing to be judged as, would change everything? What if the stories that your mind is telling you are not real? What if all you need to do is speak up or take a stand and everything will be fine? What if, even if it creates some chaos it will lead to new possibilities and all that is required is for you to go beyond it?

Chapter No. 3.3
Bio- Mimetic Mimicking

Right from the point we are conceived, we start understanding this reality to make our journey smooth. Bio-mimetic is what you lock into the body trying to duplicate or understand others. It is a natural ability of the body to be able to fit in the rest of the world. To understand means you have to stand under somebody else's universe.

Bio-mimetic mimicry is where you mimic the psychology and physiology of somebody else. And you actually lock it into your body so it's with you all the time.

You mimic the same energetic pathways, the energetic pathways create the biochemical pathways, which also create the way the structure shows up in your body, the way the emotional patterns show up in your life, the way patterns of choice or no choice show up. It's this intensity of your creative capacity continuously going into mimicking, rather than creating. You mimic others' pathways and point of views when you need to  understand them from an intellectual or energetic point of view and that requires you to lock the similarities into your body in order to have clarity from your point of view to theirs.

If you look at the way kids start looking like and behaving like their parents. We bio-mimetically mimic our parents a lot yet our parents are not the only one we mimic. The good news is it can be undone with some healing and when you heal everywhere you are mimicking others, that which is you start showing up and you start getting clarity on who you are and more importantly, you start being you. This releases a lot of frustration as most of the time we are unknowingly frustrated because we are never clear about what we really want as we are automatically thinking and feeling based on the thoughts, feeling and emotions we are mimicking while truly we do not wish to do it. This client of mine was also mimicking her parents who displayed the tendency of committing suicide in front of her when she was a kid and then when she got married unknowingly she started mimicking the same behavior of constant suicidal thoughts.

Another client of mine was Bio mimetically mimicking his father so much that he didn't even realize that he was not growing in his life because of that. When I started working with him, he realized that his father had an innate fear of failure and of loosing people that he started mimicking as he was trying to understand it while growing up. And all this was in the depth of his Magical Mind and he was not cognitively getting it. He had superb business ideas but he wasn't implementing them because he would automatically go into thoughts of "what if I fail?", "what if my family disagree to it?", "What if they leave me?" and all this was building up massive levels of frustration as he wasn't Being himself, ultimately leading to failure and thus suicidal thoughts.

Few sessions of healing (Bio-mimetic Mimicry) and he is taking charge of his life, he has started up his venture and he is shocked with the results himself.

I suggest that you learn the process of Bio mimetic mimicry by attending a 4 days Foundation Class or a 4 hours Body Process Class of Access Consciousness yet I am sharing the clearing statement of the process with you here to make a difference. It would be great if you record this and put it on a loop overnight (you can do this at zero volume, it still works).

BMM Process

What have you made so vital, valuable and real about the biomimetic and biomimetric mimicry of other people's pain, pathways and realities? Everything that is times a godzillion will you destroy and uncreate it please? **Right and wrong, good and bad, POD and POC, all 9, shorts, boys and beyonds.**

Chapter No.3.4
Entities

This is my favorite topic. Entities are beings without bodies. And they are not always the way we have seen in movies and television series. Usually they are too subtle to be noticed and also we do not pay attention to them because we believe it is unreal as we are implanted to believe that way. Yes there are beings without bodies, that couldn't go to the light for some reason and now they are stuck here as they believe they do not have a choice, yet they would like to play with beings with bodies as that's the only way they can have a human experience now.

It is though not a direct cause of suicide as no entity can make us do anything against our will yet the entities take over in cases where a person is either an addict or highly drunk or

obsessively negative thinker (remember my client had half a bottle of whisky to finally make her loose it and she was also a constant negative thinker).

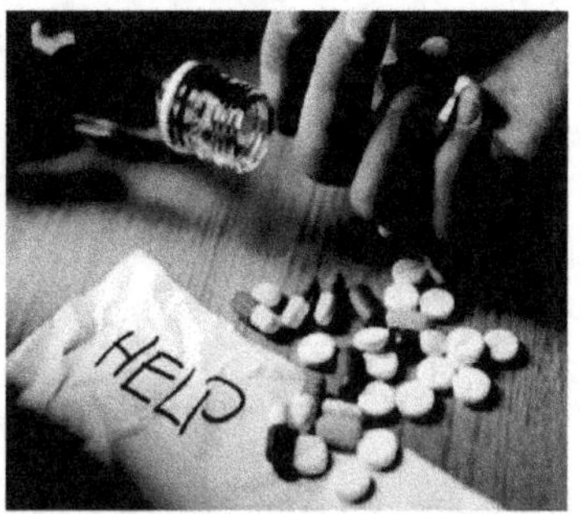

When we do not believe in our self and call for help and we do not actually ask people with body then people without body join in and start helping us, which is not scary at all as there are also entities that are contributing entities and they selflessly without any charge help us yet sometimes we may end up calling those entities that start sucking our energies, start feeding their own point of views in our head and create havoc in our life. This is the reason why it has been seen that addicts have high chances of suicide.

Let's make it simple, so what will happen if you leave your house open? Yes, some weird kind of people may enter and they will try to take over the property. Now, every time you say or think, I don't want to live here, I don't want this life, I want to run away, what happens is that the being that you are leaves the body. There is a small percentage of your energy left in your body to run your life as a major part of you decided to leave it.

Thus, what you experience is absent mindedness, tiredness, lack of energy etc. on top of all this what happens is that the beings without the body which for some reason could not go to the light jumps in and start enjoying through you. So now, along with all the other stuff you were going through-doing things you do not wish to do or thinking the way you would not truly desire (thanks to the implants and biomemetic mimicry) and having very little interest and energy to do things or live your life, you now have some additional beings in your body which would mean that now you may eat a lot or too little, you will sleep a lot or not at all, you can definitely not make decisions with ease as there are multiple voices in your head which you believe are all yours and you can't figure out which one is right, you will have difficulty having

relationships as you are already in relationship with so many of them in there. In short, total mess. Does it describe your life or does it remind you of someone?

I have had clients who have been through years of anti depressants and sleeping pills and things getting worse rather than improving and they experience instant results in the first session and immense results after few sessions.

Affirming "I am the personality in charge", does help and also being totally present. As long as you have backdoors open you are allowing the entities to take over and create havoc in your life. Taking full responsibility of yourself and your life and knowing that everything that has happened in your life was your creation begins the positive change.

Chapter No.3.5
Current Life Traumatic Experience (It's All Over Syndrome)

You just read about Entities, beings without body that are stuck because they don't 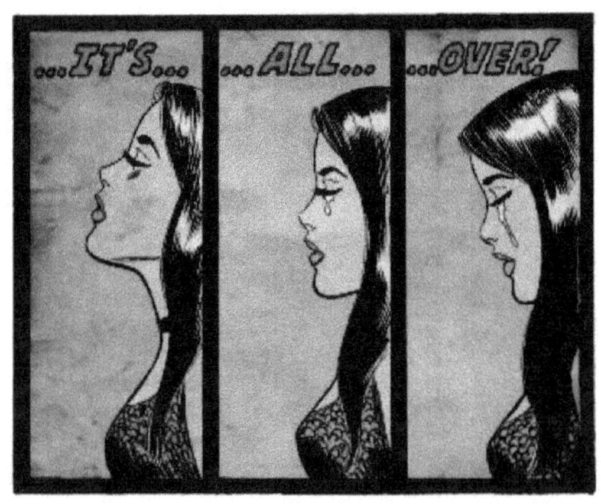

know that they are stuck or they don't believe that they have a choice to be free or to leave. Similar to that we have beings with body that are stuck in some incidence in the past and they believe that their life is over already or they do not know that they have a choice to be free from what happened. The only difference between them and us is that they do not have a body and we do. Are we also not stuck in some part of our past and believe that we cannot be free from the effect of it?

I have had clients whose boyfriends or girlfriends ditched them, some got divorced and some experienced demise of a loved one, some experienced a financial setback etc. and they believed that it is all over before coming to me. If you have ever had an experience where you felt that it's all over but you continued to survive and you are just surviving and not living your life to the fullest, do me a favour, right now? Just take a deep breath. Yes, really take a deep breath in and now in this moment know that as long as you are breathing it is never over. Don't forget to breathe out, ok. Remember, the show is on as long as the breath is on. No matter what happened, if you are still breathing there is some life yet to be explored, there is some stuff yet to be done, there is someone yet to be met, there is something that only you can create, there is some contribution that you are here for on this planet which you haven't completed yet. Ask questions, what contribution can I be on the planet? What would I like my life to be like? It is the question that will open the doors of the new possibilities not the conclusion. It's all over, is a conclusion. I can never make more money again is a conclusion. I can never have someone who will truly love me is a conclusion. I can never trust anyone now is a conclusion. What is your conclusion? Is it exciting you anymore? Would you like to give it up and start asking questions instead?

Being in Question is an amazing way to live your life. The question empowers, the answer always dis-empowers. One  of the dynamic differences of access is that it is all about being in the question, never claiming to be the answer or have the answers. Questions, unlock the places of limitation, and bring light to where you are choosing to not have choice. Being aware that the question can change the energy of any situation, you can begin to see that it is always a question that has opened up a different door, a different possibility. If you are willing to continually be the question, you open the doors of infinite possibilities.

One thing to take care of here is that "why me" is the only question we don't be. Why is a loop, it makes us coming back to similar situation. Look at your life and notice that for every situation that you had been asking "Why does this happen to me?" Doesn't it keep on happening? Universe has no point of view about what you ask and is continuously granting all your wishes, so when you say "why does it happen to me?" The molecules of the universe begin to move to create a future situation for you to have awareness by yourself about what you are asking and how will you have that awareness? You will get a similar situation, the only thing is, every time you miss the awareness you were meant to have through that situation, the consecutive situation gets more intense for you to get the awareness eventually.

And when we are living with conclusions like 'I am not good enough", "I am unlucky" etc. we refuse to ask the questions like "what's right about this?", "what is the way out?",

"What else is possible?" and thus we miss the awareness to the infinite possibilities of ease, joy and glory.

Here are some of the questions you can be-

- How does it get even better than this?
- What else is possible?
- What is it that I m refusing to be, that if I would be it will change everything?
- Who or what am I not willing to annoy?

Chapter No.3.6
Root Cause Of All Your Miseries And Its Antidote

If you observe your miseries carefully, you will find that the root of all your miseries is JUDGEMENT. You are in whicheversitueation you are (especially if it is not working for you) because you have either been judging yourself or others or you had been avoiding being judged. This distracts you from acknowledging things, people or situations for what they are and thus creates aversion or craving which eventually creates the upset. Thus, you either start running away from the discomfort or keep hoping for the pleasure.

One of the greatest tools to unlocking us from this addiction is to function from allowance. Allowance is where everything is just

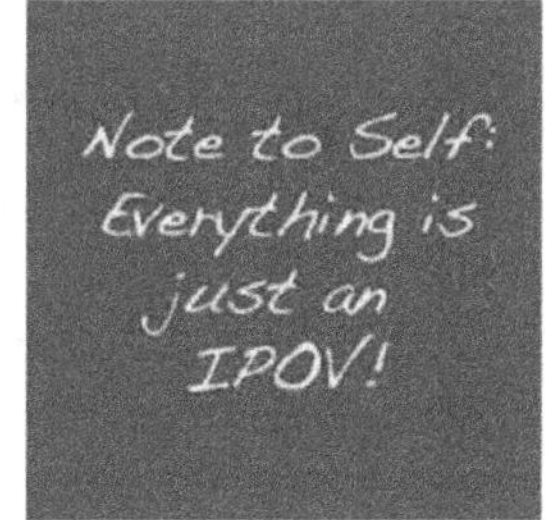

an interesting point of view. Isn't all realities that we have believed in, bought into, made real or made significant, were someone's point of view? Allowance lets us become aware of all the areas in our life where we are either aligning and agreeing or resisting and reacting to any points of view, thoughts, feelings, emotions, beliefs, judgments, conclusions or considerations. We can begin to set ourselves free by reminding ourselves that everything we think, feel, believe, judge or have decided is just an interesting point of view (IPOV).

There is one more awareness that I got that you can completely ignore as its way more weird and wacky than anything I have spoken so far. Consider that there are invisible aliens around us that are feeding on our energy and their access to us is polarity and judgment. If you notice, there is a certain energy you be in, every time your head goes into –"Should I do this or shouldn't?"; "He shouldn't have done this"; "I shouldn't have said it"; "It is wrong". And then our head takes a trip down the lane of all negative and disempowering thoughts. Consider that right at that time there is an alien around waiting to put his straw into one of your chakras (energy center) and suck energy out of you. So what to do now? STOP!! The minute you catch yourself taking a trip down the lane of judgments, STOP, make a fresh choice and ask an empowering question.

Chapter No. 3.7
Thoughts, Feelings & Emotions (Who Does It Belong? Illustrated By Dr. Dain Heer)

Will you ever commit suicide if you are so peaceful that you have no thoughts, no feelings and no emotions? You are far more psychic than you ever give yourself credit for. 98% of your thoughts feelings and emotions don't belong to you. You are like the psychic Sponge Bob of the universe.

The greatest freedom you can give yourself is to **spend three days asking: *"Who does this belong to?"*** for every thought, feeling, and emotion you have. Three days of: "Who does this belong to?" will set you free of all the thoughts, feelings and emotions other people have. It will be the most work you have ever done in your life. For every thought, feeling, and emotion you have, ask the question. If it lightens up at all, just return it to sender. It's not yours. There will be so many thoughts, feelings and emotions coming at you that after 20 minutes you'll be exhausted. By the second day, the moment you ask: "Who does this belong to?" it will go back to where it came from. You'll do it for a while, and then you'll forget, then you'll remember and you'll do it for a while and then you'll forget, and that will take care of the second day. The third day, about half way through the day, all of a sudden, you'll have no thoughts in your head, and you'll become a walking, talking meditation.

Meditation can be difficult because every time you would quiet your mind, everybody else's would get louder in your head. So you sit there going, "I have to go home and eat." But you just ate. "I have to go home and do my laundry." But you don't do your laundry. You get a quiet mind and you get to hear everybody else's louder. With, "Who does this belong to?" you'll be a walking meditation.

One question that arises here is that how do you know if it's a yes or no. The answer is very simple as when you ask yourself a question you may get that feeling of heaviness like the feeling you get when you enter in a place where someone has just had a fight, that's a straight no. Whereas when you feel lighter or you get a sense of expansion, well that's a yes. So basically these tools provide the awareness to the seekers and empower people to know what they know.

If it's not yours only two other things could be possible one is that it is someone else's and if that's light. If you are like, oh it is someone else's then you could return it to sender with consciousness attached because you don't want to stock anybody right? And in the second case if it's something else ninety nine percent of the time it is the earth requiring a contribution from us just a simple energetic contribution not our bad feelings of fear it's the energy in the potency of fear or anger or worry or whatever it's just an energy and sometimes the earth is knocking on the door like hey could you contribute back to me too. Whatever thoughts feelings and emotions you have going on, in giving it back to the earth will dissipate those feelings and all of sudden you're lighter again. How does it get even better than that?

Chapter 4
What To Do When You Have Suicidal Thoughts?

First of all, take total charge of yourself, do not get carried away by your fantasies of how you would do it and who all will be effected by it. Remember that 99% of your

thoughts, feelings and emotions are not even yours. Yes, you are like this antenna catching signals from everyone around and everything around you. Ask - who does it belong to? POC and POD (refer to page no.109 for details) everywhere you are making yourself wrong or others are making you wrong. Ask yourself what miracle you are that you are not acknowledging and also, who are you avoiding to be that if you would be it would change everything?

Most of the time people commit suicide because they think there is no way out of the situation. Remember your point of view creates your reality. When you believe that there is no way out, guess what, there will be no way out. Every time we conclude something we block any possibility to show-up. Being in the question and asking right questions opens new doors of possibilities and thus have the potency to alter any future. If you were considering suicide, it may be because something was not happening the way you decided is best for you and you concluded there is no other option. Being in question is a very powerful tool to change any reality. Question has the quality to change the molecules and create a different future.

One of my client, was in a relationship that didn't turn out the way she desired it to turn out, she had thoughts of ending it all but today I am so glad that she didn't and some of her friend suggested her to meet me. With some healing and being in the question, "what will it take for a loving being who would be a total contribution to my life and will be open to receive my contribution, to show up in my life with total ease at the speed of space?" her reality shifted. She is now married to an amazing person who loves her unconditionally and is a total contribution in her life.

Another client of mine owed a lot of money to people and he thought of taking the highway (you know what I mean) yet when I started working with him and asking him that what is it that he is refusing to be here that he can be, that if he would be it would change everything? He ended up telling all the stakeholders authentically that he is not in a position to pay it back before 2 years and also did his planning for how much money he needs to set aside and thus how much extra he has to earn to pay it off. He also started asking for more money from the universe and started destroying and uncreating everything that doesn't allow that and he actually started making more money. Ask and receive is one of the laws of the Universe. He started asking – "What can I add to my life today to make more money right away?"

What if that what you are avoiding to be, controls you?
What does it mean?

So if you have a judgment about lying and you hate those who lie and you are clear that you will never lie, guess what? You will always end up having people around you who lie and of course you won't like it.

Most of us are implanted that we must be nice as we will only get what we desire and eventually be free from all our karmas if we be nice to everyone. In the process we handicap ourselves, paralyze ourselves and diminish ourselves energetically. What if you actually have a freedom to be or do anything? What can you be that you haven't considered being because it has been made so wrong that you won't choose to be it? What if you can be nasty? What if you can be a killing energy that no one can dare to mess with? And yes when you start being that all of the sudden, some people may have problem but that is their problem not yours.

When I ask – what if you can be... I do not mean you have to be it. I am only saying that you have a choice to be it too. It's surprising how only those who may never harm anyone fear that if they would be out of control or form or structure or significance, they may end up being EVIL (or harm someone) and those who are EVIL would not have this fear as they are anyways doing it already and they are righteous about it. Yet, it is time that the "nice" people on the planet wear their hiss, take the charge and come out of their victim mode.

Is it truly the time to come out of your victim mode?

If you have been playing victim in your life, trust me, it has been serving you in one way or the other. It either helps you to avoid responsibility, or allows you to simply do nothing, or gets you attention or sympathy or helps you to maintain the status quo of the eutopian ideal of this reality or maintain your perfect image in front of some people or whatever but it is definitely serving you something. Now, what would it take for you to be brutally honest with yourself and acknowledge that whatever is your payoff, is it worth it? Is it worth your life?

What all will be available to you, if you stop getting lured by the little perks you are deriving from playing the victim? What if your life is not nearly as f*cked up as you pretend it to be? What if you are far more potent to create a situation where you are being victimized and if you can create this, what else can you create?

Vent it Out

If you are having thoughts of self-doubt, disbelief, hopelessness or quitting it is always a good idea to take them out and not let them stew inside of you to explode. Now you can vent it out by screaming into your pillow or crying or writing it all on a paper and then tearing it into small pieces and flushing it or sharing it with someone who is a good listener and who doesn't judge you. Be vulnerable.

I attended a self-development course once, it was my first course of such kind and my biggest breakthrough was – that what I had kept in my heart as a secret, that I thought I shouldn't tell anyone as no one will understand, was not a secret there were so many who had similar issues. When we make incidences of our life secret, they kind of haunt us and if we make them infinite, they stop having the charge. Now, look at me for years I didn't let anyone know that I had been dealing with suicidal thoughts now I have made it so infinite that the whole world would know it. What if that one secret that you are holding on to can be a contribution to the planet and it may sound obnoxious to your logical mind but yes, that is exactly how it works. Rather than being sucked by it ask – What is right about this that I am not getting? How can this be a contribution in my life? And how does it get even better than this too?

Chapter 5
When Someone You Know
Has Suicidal Tendency

First of all, all these beings who are on a mission to commit suicide do not generally let you know. It is rare that they go around telling people that they are plotting their death. Some people may keep their thoughts and plans for suicide to themselves, which makes helping them very difficult. However, those considering suicide sometimes show signs that they are thinking, preparing, or seeking the means to carry it out. **Some suicide warning signs** include:

- Appearing agitated, anxious, irritable
- Becoming extremely sensitive and strongly reactive to criticism

- Talking, writing, journaling or joking about suicide
- Making statements like "I'd be better off dead", "I wish I was never born", "Your life would be so much better without me", "I feel like I'm just taking up space."
- Saying what sounds like a final goodbye
- Seeking out the means to kill themselves – a weapon, substance, or dangerous location
- Giving away prized possessions/ making a will or other final arrangements.
- Withdrawal from friends/ family or other major behavioral changes.
- Dropping out of group activities.
- Personality changes such as nervousness, outbursts of anger, impulsive or reckless behavior, or apathy about appearance or health.
- Frequent irritability or unexplained crying.
- Lingering expressions of unworthiness or failure.
- Lack of interest in the future.

Attempted or completed suicides happen without warning. It is a myth that asking questions will increase the chance of people harming themselves. Asking questions shows you care. One of the most important things you can offer — as a therapist, family member, bystander or friend — is being a living proof that someone cares. People start thinking of suicide when they feel hopeless and alone in their struggle. They do not see a way out. Telling them they are not alone — and really meaning it — is huge. They desperately need someone to care.

Here are some questions you can ask:

- "You seem really depressed lately – how are you handling that? Getting help?"
- "What do you think about your future?"
- "Have you thought about doing something about that?"

If you suspects that a friend or family member is considering suicide, what should you do?

There are three very important things to do if you notice the warning signs for suicide or the young person tells you  directly that they are thinking about suicide. The first thing is to always show the person that you are concerned about them – listen without judgment, ask about their feelings and avoid trying to come up with a solution to their problem. LISTEN to them, be the space of no-judgment and be a stand for them to choose to be themselves. They are planning to quit because this life doesn't seem like a playground where they can live fully and be themselves, anymore. Can you be a different possibility for them? Can you be an inspiration for them to realize that joy is possible?

If you are in relationship with someone and you are fearful they might

hurt themselves, tell them so. You can say,

- "I am concerned about you."
- "I care about you."

Tell your loved one why you are concerned. Listen. Offer to help them get support. Remind them they are not alone, you care!

Call a facilitator as soon as possible. You will need support to take good care of yourself and your loved one. Your loved one will need help to evaluate and treat their depression. A person who feels enough emotional pain to make desperate statements needs someone to assist them in getting support. It is true that a person can talk of dying, and not intend to take his or her own life. But a suicide attempt or suicidal ideation are not mere stunts for attention. They are important ways people communicate dangerous levels of distress. Many of us need to know how to respond. Also, if you are dealing with someone who is suicidal then there are following things you can be careful about-

- Never give them lecture how they "should" be.
- Be a good Listener. This involves listening without judging.
- Please do not judge them or their behavior as wrong.
- Telling them that it's NOT their fault, does help.
- Making them drink water may also help.
- No matter what, do not get angry at them.
- Tell them how important they are and no matter what, everything will be alright.
- Run their Bars. (refer to Chapter 6 for details)

Chapter 6
Coping With Loved One's Demise (Dr. Anthony Mattis)

Besides the fact that I completed the book and everything was set to bring the book to fruition, the book just wasn't coming to actualization so one day I connected with the energy of the book and asked-what is it that you require that I am not acknowledging? And right then the World Suicide Prevention week came and I heard a live conversation with Dr. Anthony Mattis where he was sharing his experience of losing his wife to Suicide and how they cope with it as a family. Right then I knew that this is it; this is what the book is asking for. So I contacted Dr. Anthony and he was delighted to contribute to the book.

Dr Anthony Mattis is an Access Consciousness Facilitator, a naturopath, a chiropractor and a wonderful being. He shared - "I had some really close experience with suicide. I and my first wife were practicing different modalities and even spiritual practices for ten years but that could not prevent my wife from committing suicide as she suffered from bipolar disorder also known as manic depression. When my wife decided to leave us our kids were very young, one was just two and a half years old and other two were eight years old and ten years old. Further my financial issues added to our adversities. I was completely shattered and disheartened. Then the tools of Access Consciousness came into my life and magic was created. At first I was sort of like yeah right here I go again just another modality and of course they think this is the right way or the best way.

However after using the tools, I was amazed as the results were so profound. I experienced the immense level of intensity and power in the energetic tools of Access Consciousness. Now, my second wife and children ask me to get their bars run whenever they feel that something is not right. Just because they have experienced enough sessions to know that getting their bars run will heal all of their problems.

As soon as Access came into our life we decided that this is what we're going to do because we knew that mental illness runs strong in the family and I do believe that this tool has the potential and power to actually rewrite the D.N.A. script. That was the time I finally realized that people who are struggling with depression, chronic fatigue syndrome, insomnia, bipolar, schizophrenia can create a different possibility in their lives. They just have to be willing to choose it. Access Consciousness tools also helped my children and myself in improving our confidence, self-esteem and most importantly our outlook on life started to change even when things were down.

Access Consciousness Bars is an amazing hands on tool in which you just gently place your hands on these thirty two points on your head. All these points carry the electromagnetic components of your thoughts, feelings, beliefs and considerations in the areas of sadness, joy, creativity, body, sexuality, money and the list goes on and on. And just by touching them gently, you release blockages of thousands of years even life times.

In today's time we're always in a rush and have deadlines to meet. In this hectic schedule just laying down and getting your bars run creates changes in the brain waves. Thus, just relaxing and falling asleep during a session can change your life.

What if, when you feel down, there is nothing wrong with you but rather you are just aware of someone around you being down. Access tools begin to make you acknowledge that there is nothing wrong with you, you are sensitive to the environment and also make you get present to the places where you misidentify and misapply that you are the one who is sad or down. We fail to understand that if twenty people around us are actually sad and struggling so it is possible that actually we've been buying their reality.

What the bars start to do is, it starts to remove anywhere and everywhere, you may be functioning like that unconsciously. When you start to get your bars run, it's like the light of awareness exposes in your life.

As a father many times I have faced such situations where my kids required my advice but I didn't have any words to advice. In such situations when there are no words to change a situation just being able to lie down and receive the bars changes everything. So many time, I would say ninety eight percent of the time, when you have no words or advice to give to a person the best you can do for them is run their bars to make them feel better and it changes everything. As a practitioner I've never been more confident in the bars and the tools of access consciousness. There are so many of them and they can completely change your whole reality and I'm very grateful for it. Looks like, this can save lives and I never thought that way about any other modality out there this can truly save people's lives.

Many people are considered as insane and inappropriate for living in the world around them. One thing about people who struggle with mental illness is that they're very aware people or some people say sensitive. There is a kind of standpoint where they let people walk all over them but actually they're sensitive to the subtle energies around them. A lot of them are misidentifying and misapplying those subtle energies as their own thoughts and feelings so they start to feel like they're going crazy so that's what is beautiful about the bars and asking Who does belong to because a lot of people with mental illness are like super-duper aware beings that have a huge aptitude for different energies around them and that's one of the things I've seen with the tools of Access Consciousness. Taking something that can feel like a curse, that sensitivity, the empathy - what if it's none of those labels, it's not even mental illness? What if it's something you can really change? What if you can take something that you may have been seeing as a curse and really change and see that as a gift?

In today's times many medical doctors are putting children at eight, nine, ten years old on anti-depressants. I'm like really??!! What if you just have a really aware child? What if they're trying to pull out the sadness or the anger or the fear or the worries out of mom and dad but you just don't know how to articulate it right? So it shows up all weird or depressive in their world. What if you just have an aware child? So I would like to say to all the parents because I had this point of view that even if you think you're a lost case, get your kids in Place because it cannot only change and save your kid's life but I promise you as a parent your life will change too.

I (Shree Dembla) am in immense Gratitude to Dr. Anthony Mattis for sharing his life with my readers and I vouch every word he wrote. Just to add on, as I felt it is important to share this information here that any Access Consciousness Class around the world in free for a child accompanied by a paid adult parent. I believe it's a gift to the planet from Gary Douglas the founder of Access Consciousness as this encourages many parents to bring their kids to access classes. Many times I have seen parents going into conversations like – "My kid is too young to get it." "Will my child understand all this?" Trust me, kids get it better than adults. My youngest participants had been 4 years old & they run amazing bars & use the tools too.

Chapter 7
Myths Around Suicide

Myth No. 1
Suicide will set me free

The underlying reason behind any suicide is that the person could not bear it anymore and they think that committing suicide will end it all. However, it never happens that way. The state of being remains the same even after committing suicide. It is just the body that dies, the being either gets stuck in this realm and yet experiences the same energy which they were in before committing suicide or move on and take the birth but attract the similar kind of life where the similar experiences prevails which may eventually lead to similar actions thus resulting in suicide or suicidal thoughts in many lives until the being choose to be aware and thus be free.

Myth No. 2
You will keep hanging around after suicide

Yes, most of the time the beings keep hanging around thus this belief system prevailed however, these are those beings who had a desire to check who all will be upset with their death or what will happen to someone or some people specifically after they are gone. Having said that, there are beings that move ahead and take up a life yet their point of views may still continue and thus create similar reality for them, until they get the awareness that they always have Choice.

Myth No. 3
Talking about suicide or asking someone if they feel suicidal will encourage suicide attempts.

The first step in encouraging a suicidal person to live comes from talking about those feelings. That first step can be the simple inquiry about whether or not the person is intending to end their life. I think one has to let go of one's own judgments about suicide before talking to such person as no possibility can emerge from judgment. Allowance again is the key, being in allowance of whatever that person is concluding and yet being a stand for different choices creates a completely different space in which the person can authentically share without any hesitation and also get the awareness for themselves.

One of my friend once shared with me that her father once told her that he is contemplating committing suicide and her response was, "Dad I have always trusted you for everything and if this is what you are choosing for yourself I am with you, however, are you really choosing it or are you concluding that this is the only way out?" And she was not being sarcastic she was being a stand inside of which he shared whatever he was dealing with and they came up with other ways out and it has been years now and he is now thriving and not just surviving.

Myth No. 4
A promise to keep a note unopened and unread should always be kept.

A sealed note with the request for the note not to be opened is a very strong indicator that something is seriously amiss. A sealed note is a late sign in the progression towards suicide. If someone gives you a sealed note and says "you would know when will be the time to open it" PLEASE OPEN IT ASAP.

Myth No.5
Once a person is intent on suicide, there is no way of stopping them.

Suicides can be prevented. People can be helped.

Myth No.6
People who threaten suicide are just seeking attention.

All suicide attempts must be treated as though the person has the intent to die. Do not dismiss a suicide attempt as simply being an attention-gaining device. It is likely that the person has tried to gain attention and, therefore, this attention is needed. The attention that they get may well save their lives.

Myth No.7
Suicide is hereditary.

I have had clients who had a family history of suicide. This can be due to bio-mimetic mimicry or implants or also because the spirit of the ancestor not being released and thus creating similar thoughts or vibrations. Yet, it is not necessary that if there had been a suicide in the family, it will be carried forward as a genetic or hereditary problem.

Myth No.8
Only certain types of people become suicidal.

Everyone has the tendency for suicide. The evidence is that predisposing conditions may lead to either attempted or completed suicides. It is unlikely that those who do not have the predisposing conditions like- depression, conduct disorder, substance abuse, feeling of rejection, rage, emotional pain and anger will complete suicide.

Myth No. 9
Once a person is suicidal, they will be suicidal forever.

Most people who are considering suicide will only be that way for a limited period of their lives. Given proper assistance and support, they will probably recover and continue to lead meaningful and happy lives unhindered by suicidal concerns.

Myth No. 10
Suicidal people cannot help themselves.

While contemplating suicide, people may have a distorted perception of their actual life situation and what solutions are appropriate for them to take. However, with support and constructive assistance from caring and informed people around them, such people can gain full self-direction and self-management in their lives.

Myth No. 11
Suicidal people are always angry when someone intervenes and they will resent that person afterwards.

While it is common for people to be defensive and resist help at first, these behaviors are often barriers imposed to test how much people care and are prepared to help. For most people considering suicide, it is a relief, to have someone genuinely care about them and to be able to share the emotional burden of their plight with another person. When questioned some time later, the vast majority express gratitude for the intervention.

Myth No. 12
Suicidal people are insane or mentally ill.

Although suicidal people are likely to be extremely unhappy and may be classified as having a mood disorder, such as depression, most are not legally insane. Most of them need to be listened to and cared for.

Epilogue
Please Don't Die, The World Needs You

It took a lot of courage for me to write this book. Through the course of writing this book I personally sensed and experienced what every being who consider committing suicide go through and trust me it is not an easy space to be in, yet I knew I need to do it. I need to write this book to tell you that **if you can commit to your life, you need not commit suicide.**

"Please don't die the world needs you". These words echoed in my ears for days, months and years and kept me moving. I became a completely different person. There was some magic about these classes of Access Consciousness that I cannot cognitively figure out how it happened but it just did that I started living a totally different reality. A reality which I was not even visualizing because it was way beyond the realms of my logical mind. I have come a long way with Access Consciousness, from who I was- someone who used to wake up every morning thinking and asking- Is it worth living? To who I am today, someone who wakes up every morning with a question – "who am I choosing to be today and what grand and glorious adventure will I have today?"

And the funny thing is everything was fine in my life (apparently), I had an amazing husband and in-laws, and money was not always that big an issue, Health was all right too (seemingly) yet there was this feeling of something missing.

Gradually, through the clearing statements, access classes, body processes etc. I just started unleashing the real me, that was hidden and buried under all of those point of views and implants. And I started discovering that no matter what universe always has my back. It always did actually. Whatever I had been asking for in my life it has been providing me. And it was all about the choices. It has always been about the CHOICE.

And one pearl of possibility that I have received from Access Consciousness is "Being in Question". Question just interrupts the status quo. It just interrupts whatever we have decided it is meant to be. It just interrupts all the algorithm we have created or all the futures we have decided are only possible and right from there the possibilities show up. So when we ask a different question and we be in the awareness of the new possibilities that are showing up, we create a different future for ourselves.

What if all you need to do is choose and what if you are never wrong? Never. If you can just give that up (making yourself wrong) and you do not have to buy into other people's point a few when they are making you wrong and you can be in total gratitude for yourself and for everybody around you- those who gave you a pleasant experience and even those who created discomfort for you as both are a contribution in their own way, you will start living a different reality.

We create everything that shows up in our life the good, the bad, the ugly and the ugliest. Everything that we are choosing today is creating our future and everything that we have chosen in the past is creating our present which was a future then. Yet, we can be free from those choices that we don't even remember we have made in the past & are effecting our present. We can make fresh choices today.

So every time you make yourself wrong or you are buying into someone else's judgment of you just ask - What miracle are you that you are not acknowledging? What gift and contribution are you that you are not acknowledging? And what would it take for you to acknowledge it? Because it's only when you acknowledge it you can actualize it.

Always remember that you chose to take a body and come to this planet to experience something, to contribute something and as long as you're breathing there is some possibility unexplored, some contribution you can be to this planet that you haven't acknowledged yet. What would it take for you to be that? And what would it take for - All of life to come to you with ease and joy and glory®. All the best my friend, it's a beautiful life full of possibilities moment by moment by moment and trust me universe always has your back so just start asking and changing the molecules of the universe for the new possibilities to show up and the new possibilities will definitely show up.

By the way, that client of mine has started her own cookery classes from her own house, she also does Access Consciousness Classes, is in immense love for herself, respect herself and others and live her life fully.

Take care of yourself, my friend. Rock your life and be the killing energy. Looking forward to see you in person someday and please do write to me at connect@shreedembla.com or www.shreedembla.com/pleasedontdie , I would love to hear from you. Please share - how this book has been a contribution in your life and also if there is any further queries.

You can find me on Facebook at www.facebook.com/shreedembla9999 and you can even check my website for latest updates @ www.shreedembla.com. I would love to see you, hear from you, meet you and contribute to your life in whichever way I would.

Please Don't Die,
The World Needs You!!

When the things don't go as you
thought they would. When you are
torn apart between what you want
and what you should.

When your scream is so loud
that it echoes in your mind yet,
more silent than a whisper,
shhh... the world shouldn't find.

When you are wondering whom to speak to,
as no one understands.
When you are sick of taking efforts & all
your hope seems to come to an end.

When there is nowhere to run as
What's killing you are the voices in your own
head.These thoughts and images that wait for
you to be alone and then attack.

Saying that you should just give up and stop
trying, SHUT UP & let me live, I shout;
You shut up & listen they say, it's all over

and the only way to be free is the way out.

They grew louder and
denser the more I fought
So I surrendered as there is no
point fighting myself I thought.

Years I spent in pain,
suffering and solitude,
And then I found a secret recipe of Ease, Joy,
Allowance & Gratitude.

Fighting with these thoughts, fuel them
further I found.
Being in allowance with them, gives me
strength to go around.

Being aware that these thoughts
are not who I am, was the first step to
freedom. POCing & PODing them
as they arose lead to different creation.

Sending them back to the sender
has become so much fun.
That now I awake up with
enthusiasm to see the morning Sun.

The world needs more people like me,
now I have found.
Not even a moment I shall waste
in self judgment and doubt.

I now choose to strut my wings to fly,
As he (Dr. Dain Heer) once told me,
Shree "the world needs you, please don't Die".
  & Here I am telling you with sparkling eyes
  & Yes the world needs You, Please Don't Die.

Clearing Statement - A Potent Tool for Change and Transformation

What if a few weird words could totally change your life?

If you are around people who have done Access Consciousness classes or tele-calls, you are likely to hear them say this weird thing that sounds totally like a foreign language, or maybe you won't even hear it because your brain has just turned into mush! (In case you're wondering... this is a really good thing – it means the clearing statement is working its magic on you).

Many modalities clear the limitations built around words. Access Consciousness clears the energy underneath the words. Much of what we would like to change is not cognitive or logical; it is created and held energetically. Take a moment to recall a time when you got really angry about something without being clear about the logical reason... was it actually an energy you were aware of?

The beauty, magic and potency of the Access Consciousness Clearing Statement is its capacity to clear the hidden stuff that you aren't even aware of that is keeping you stuck! So, you don't need to go through the pain, suffering and gory of reliving a situation to clear the charge on it! How does it get even better than that?

So, when you ask a question or think about something that is limiting you or not working for you, there is an energy that comes up. It's a lot like defragging a computer. The energy comes up, you run the clearing statement and then you have a whole lot more space from which to create anything you choose!

These crazy weird words are the Access Consciousness Clearing Statement – a simple tool that thousands of people around the world use every day to continually create a life of ease, joy and glory. You can use it to change almost anything that is keeping you stuck, limited or tied up in knots!

Right & Wrong, Good & Bad:

What's good, perfect and correct about this?

What's wrong, mean, vicious, terrible, bad, and awful about this?

What's right and wrong, good and bad?

POC:

Is the point of creation of the thoughts, feelings and emotions immediately preceding whatever you decided?

POD:

Is the point of destruction immediately following whatever you decided? It's like pulling the bottom card out of a house of cards. The whole thing falls down.

All 9:

Stands for nine layers of crap that we're taking out. You know that somewhere in those nine layers, there's got to be a pony because you couldn't put that much crap in one place without having a pony in there. It's crap that you're generating yourself, which is the bad part. You created it, you can change it.

Shorts:

Is the short version of: What's meaningful about this? What's meaningless about this? What's the punishment for this? What's the reward for this?

Boys:

Stands for nucleated spheres. Have you ever been told you have to peel the layers of the onion to get to the core of an issue? Well, this is it—except it's not an onion. It's an energetic structure that looks like one. These are pre-verbal.

Have you ever seen one of those kids' bubble pipes? Blow here and you create a mass of bubbles on the other end of the pipe? As you pop one bubble it fills back in. Basically these have to do with those areas of our life where we've tried to change something continuously with no effect. This is what keeps something repeating ad infinitum...

Beyonds:

Are feelings or sensations you get that stop your heart, stop your breath, or stop your willingness to look at possibilities. It's like when your business is in the red and you get another final notice and you say argh! You weren't expecting that right now.

– And sometimes we just say, "POC and POD it. Source – Access Consciousness website

Bonus Clearings for You

All your expectations, projections, conclusions, rejections, separations, decisions and judgments about this book, what it will change, what it won't change and also all your projections, expectations, separation, rejections, conclusions, decisions and judgments of me, can we please destroy and uncreate them all?

Right and Wrong, Good and Bad, POD and POC All 9 Shorts Boys and Beyonds.

All the promises, vows, oaths, commitments, commealities, fealities, bindings, bonding contracts that you made to yourself or to others in this lifetime or in any other lifetime, across all time space dimensions & realities, will you now revoke, recant, reclaim, rescind, renounce, denounce destroy and uncreate it all.

Right and Wrong, Good and Bad, POD and POC All 9 Shorts Boys and Beyonds.

How many promises, vows, oaths, commitments, commealties, fealities, swearings, bindings and bonding contracts do you have to everything you have oaths, vows fealities, commealties, swearings, commitments, promises and contracts to throughout all times, space, dimensions and realities, and bodies, minds and lifetimes that keeps you from having total choice as your reality? All of those, will you please revoke, recant, rescind, reclaim, renounce, denounce, destroy and uncreate them all?

Right and wrong, good and bad, POD and POC, all 9, shorts, boys and beyonds.

Everywhere you had been cursed and everywhere you cursed someone and you made it real, would you please revoke, recant, rescind, reclaim, renounce, denounce, destroy and uncreate it all?

Right and Wrong, Good and Bad, POD and POC, All 9, Shorts, Boys and Beyonds.

What have you made so vital, valuable and real about the biomimetic and biomimetric mimicry of other people's pain, pathways and realities? Everything that is times a godzillion will you destroy and uncreate it please?

Right and wrong, good and bad, POD and POC, all 9, shorts, boys and beyonds.

All your expectations, projections, conclusions, rejections, separations, decisions and judgments about you with regards to your life, can you please destroy and uncreate it all?

Right and Wrong, Good and Bad, POD and POC All 9 Shorts Boys and Beyonds.

All your expectations, projections, conclusions, rejections, separations, decisions and judgments of others about you from this life or any other life time, will you please destroy and uncreate it all?

Right and Wrong, Good and Bad, POD and POC All 9 Shorts Boys and Beyonds.

I am dying to go for a holiday, I am dying to take a break, I am dying to eat good food, I am dying to get married, I am dying to get divorced, I am dying to have child, I am dying to see my children to grow up, Everything this is, can we please destroy and uncreate this?

Right and Wrong, Good and Bad, POD and POC All 9 Shorts Boys and Beyonds.

Everywhere you still think that you won't be potent enough and powerful enough to change things and you have to die to control. Can you please destroy and uncreate it all?

Right and Wrong, Good and Bad, POD and POC All 9 Shorts Boys and Beyonds.

Everywhere control is not a choice, everywhere you have already concluded everything that's already out of your control, will you please destroy and uncreate it all?

Right and Wrong, Good and Bad, POD and POC All 9 Shorts Boys and Beyonds.

Where ever you have ever sabotaged yourself and everywhere you are still doing it, will you please destroy and uncreate it all?

Right and Wrong, Good and Bad, POD and POC All 9 Shorts Boys and Beyonds.

Everywhere you are dying in bits and pieces and dying in little quantities everyday will you be please willing to destroy and uncreate it all?

Right and Wrong, Good and Bad, POD and POC All 9 Shorts Boys and Beyonds.

Everywhere you said that ultimately we have to die, ultimately you have to leave this body, so ultimately there is no point really, that's the ultimate destination that everywhere you have made it your ultimate goal of life. Can you please destroy and uncreate it all?

Right and Wrong, Good and Bad, POD and POC All 9 Shorts Boys and Beyonds.

How many oaths, vows, swearing, fealities, commealities, commitements, bindings, bonding contracts to yourself or any or all beings to give up your life, to actually die and to end your life will you please revoke, recant, rescind, reclaim,, renounce, denounce, destroy and uncreate it all?

Right and Wrong, Good and Bad, POD and POC All 9 Shorts Boys and Beyonds.

What grand and glorious adventures can you have today? What Miracle are you that you haven't acknowledged yet? Everything that doesn't allow it destroy and uncreate it times a Godzillion.

Right and Wrong, Good and Bad, POD and POC All 9 Shorts Boys and Beyonds.

What have you made so vital, valuable and real that is making you create all the limitations of this reality instead of creating a new reality? Everything that is will you destroy and uncreate it all.

Right and Wrong, Good and Bad, POD and POC All 9 Shorts Boys and Beyonds.

What have you made so vital, valuable and real about being a creator at crap instead of a miracle? Everything that is destroy and uncreate it times a Godzillion.

Right and Wrong, Good and Bad, POD and POC All 9 Shorts Boys and Beyonds.

What have you made so vital, valuable and real about the causal incarceration, causal incarnation and causal inculcation that create everything you cannot change in my reality?

Everything that is destroy and uncreate it times a Godzillion.

Right and Wrong, Good and Bad, POD and POC All 9 Shorts Boys and Beyonds.

Everywhere you are limiting yourself and making yourself small to fit into others' realities to keep them happy, destroy and uncreate it all.

Right and Wrong, Good and Bad, POD and POC All 9 Shorts Boys and Beyonds.

What invention are you using to create the abuse you are choosing? Everything that is destroy and uncreate it times a Godzillion.

Right and Wrong, Good and Bad, POD and POC All 9 Shorts Boys and Beyonds.

How much unconsciousness are you using to buy, live and sustain the lies of this reality with respect to your money, relationships and body are you choosing?

Everything that is destroy and uncreate it times a Godzillion.

Right and Wrong, Good and Bad, POD and POC All 9 Shorts Boys and Beyonds.

What are you refusing to be that is you would be it, will change everything? Everything that doesn't allow it destroy and uncreate it times a Godzillion.

Right and Wrong, Good and Bad, POD and POC All 9 Shorts Boys and Beyonds.

What age did you choose to fail? What age are you being right now? Everywhere you made failing or avoiding to fail or not failing your reality. Everything that is destroy and uncreate it times a Godzillion.

Right and Wrong, Good and Bad, POD and POC All 9 Shorts Boys and Beyonds.

How much of yourself did you destroy to validate your decisions and conclusions that you were right or wrong or someone else was right or wrong and everything you are still doing to validate it, will you destroy and uncreate it all?

Right and Wrong, Good and Bad, POD and POC All 9 Shorts Boys and Beyonds.

All the implants & explants of joy being wrong & sadness right will you destroy and uncreate it all.

Right and Wrong, Good and Bad, POD and POC All 9 Shorts Boys and Beyonds.

What if happiness, joy and bliss is your birth right?

What if ease, joy and glory is possible and available?

Everything that doesn't all that, will you destroy and uncreate all that?

Right and Wrong, Good and Bad, POD and POC All 9 Shorts Boys and Beyonds.

All of Life Comes to me with Ease Joy & Glory! ® (What contribution will be using this

10 times in the morning and 10 times in the
evening be?)

115